This book ~~belongs to:~~
is shared with

Finn and Willa
Happy Valentine's
Day! Love,
Grammie &
Papa

the hug who got stuck

to all who hug

© July 2020 Conscious Stories LLC

Illustrations by Alexis Aronson

Published by
Conscious Stories LLC
1831 12th Ave South, Suite 118
Nashville, TN 37203

www.consciousstories.com

First Edition
Library of Congress
Control Number: 2017901959

ISBN 978-1-943750-05-4

The last 20 minutes of every day are precious.

Dear parents, teachers, and readers,

This story has been gift-wrapped with two simple mindfulness practices to help you connect more deeply with your children in the last 20 minutes of each day.

● Quietly set your intention for calm and open connection.

● Then start your story time with the **Snuggle Breathing Meditation**. Read each line aloud and take slow deep breaths together. This can be very relaxing and help everyone settle.

● At the end of the story, you will find your **Daily Hug Meter**. If your children (or you) are low on hugs for the day, now is the time to catch up before sleep. It is also an opportunity to remember the people whom you loved today and those you are going to give love to tomorrow. Please don't skip this. It helps to create belonging and heal feelings of loneliness.

Enjoy snuggling into togetherness!

Andrew

Snuggle Breathing

Our story begins with us breathing together.
Say each line aloud and then
take a slow deep breath in and out.

I breathe for me

I breathe for you

I breathe for us

I breathe for all that surrounds us

Once upon a time,
on a very ordinary day,
deep in the center
of a very ordinary heart ...

an...

extraordinary...

thing...

happened.

③

Deep in the center
of this heart
was a Hug Factory.

The Hug Factory
made the most warm,
cozy, cuddly hugs.

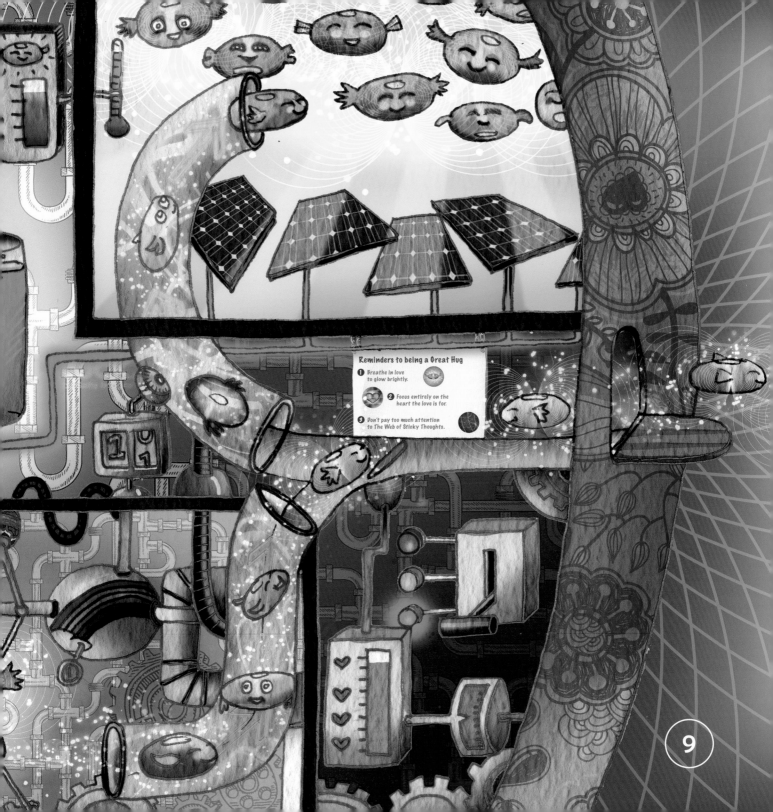

Reminders to being a Great Hug

1 Breathe in love to glow brightly.

2 Focus entirely on the heart the love is for.

3 Don't pay too much attention to The Web of Sticky Thoughts.

9

Each hug was freshly made
and specially encoded
with just the right amount
of love and care
to delight the heart
it was made for.

Being a hug wasn't always easy.

Sometimes a lonely thought
or bad feeling would trap
a hug in a sticky web.

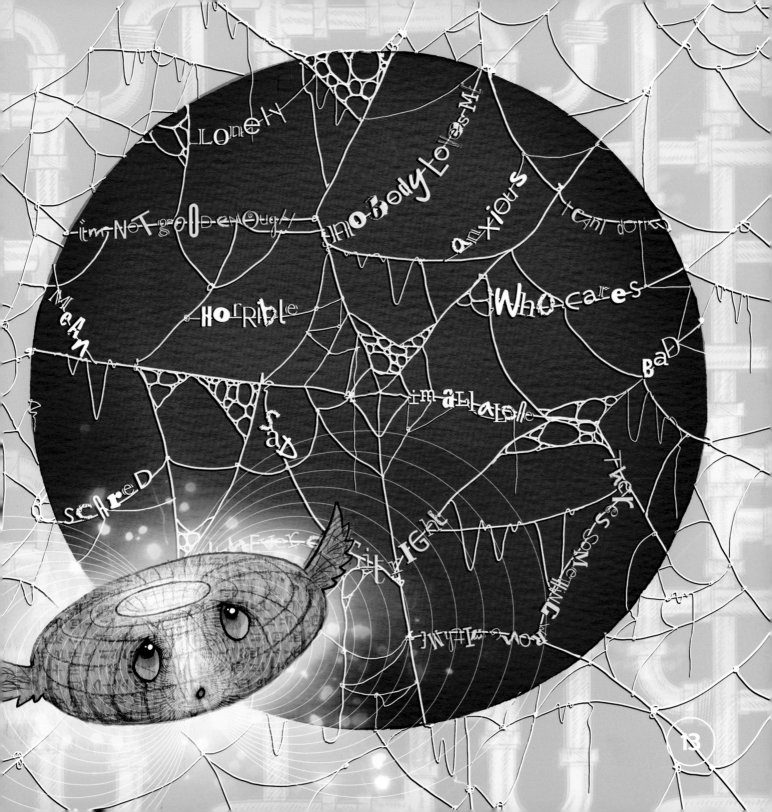

So, to help hugs deliver their love and care, there was a big sign on the factory wall:

Reminders to being a Great Hug

1 Breathe in love to glow brightly.

2 Focus entirely on the heart the love is for.

3 Don't pay too much attention to The Web of Sticky Thoughts.

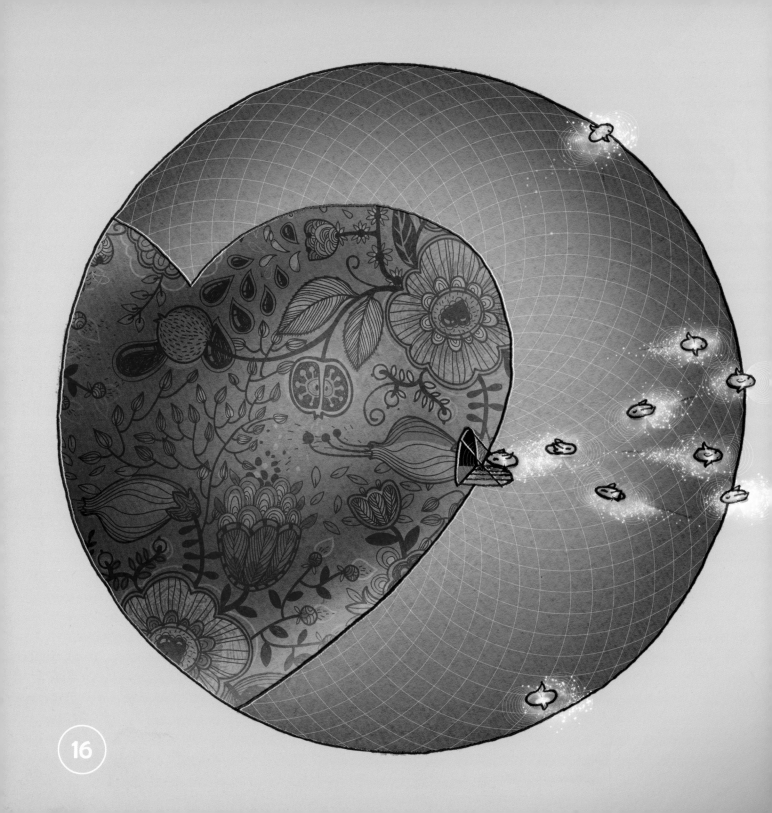

On most days you could see
streams of hugs entering and
leaving the door of the heart,
zooming away like bees from
a hive, but not on this day.

On this day there was
a problem ...

One special hug, on its way out of the heart, got stuck.

Very, very stuck.

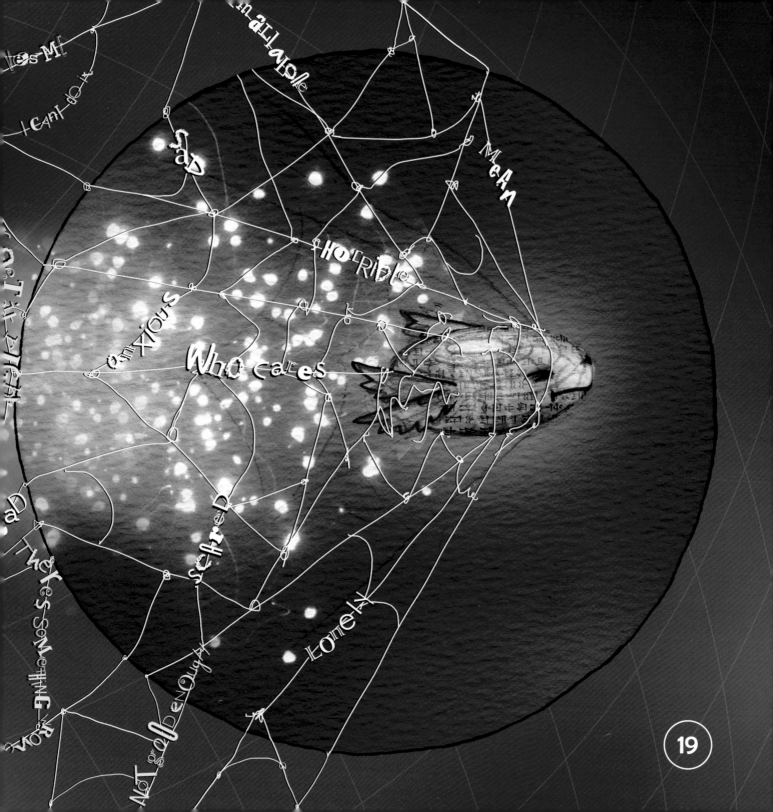

19

This hug had forgotten
the third rule!

It fought against The Web of
Sticky Thoughts to get free,
but every wriggle and squirm
trapped the hug even more.

Soon the hug
ran out of breath
and lost its glow.

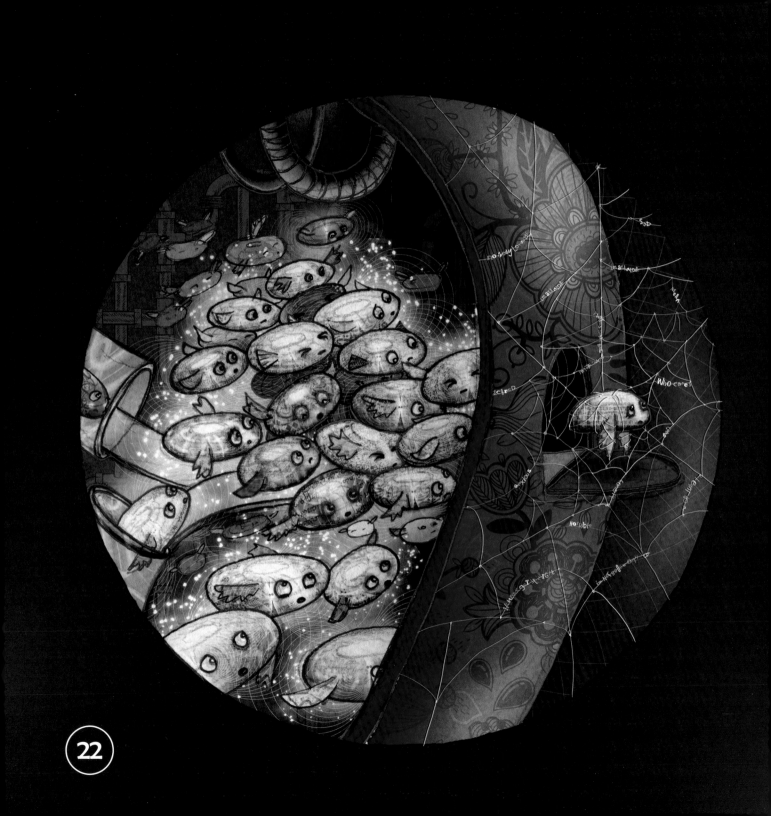

Inside, the heart became
horribly congested with crowds
of hugs waiting to get out.

Unused hugs were put into
boxes until every inch of space
was *filled up.*

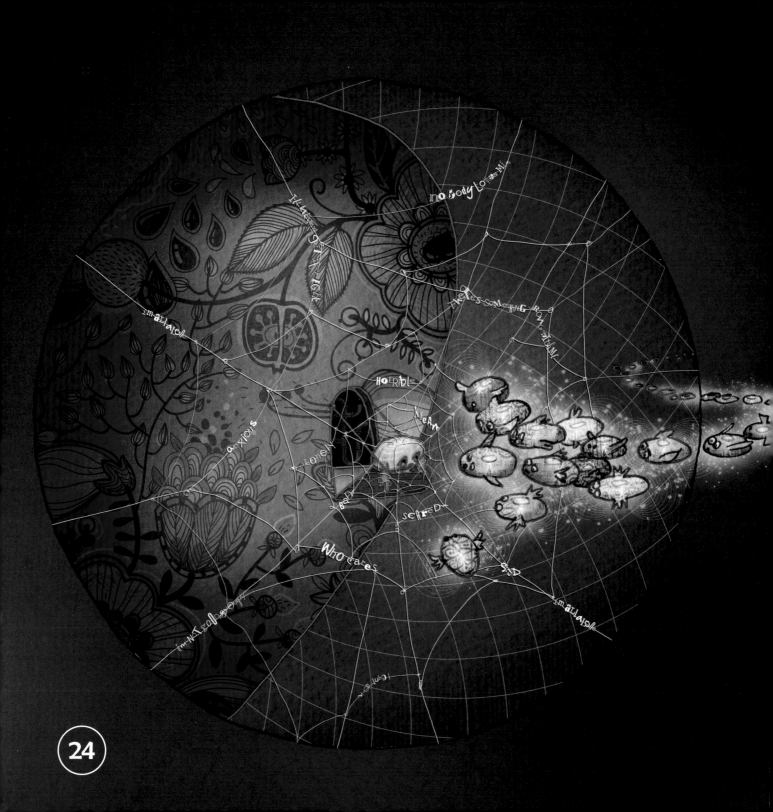

Outside the heart there
was also a problem.

A traffic jam of visiting hugs
couldn't get in to deliver their
special love and care.

Soon the factory
stopped making
new hugs.

There was only one stuck hug
in the center of one ordinary
heart, but all around the world,
hugs lost a little of their glow.

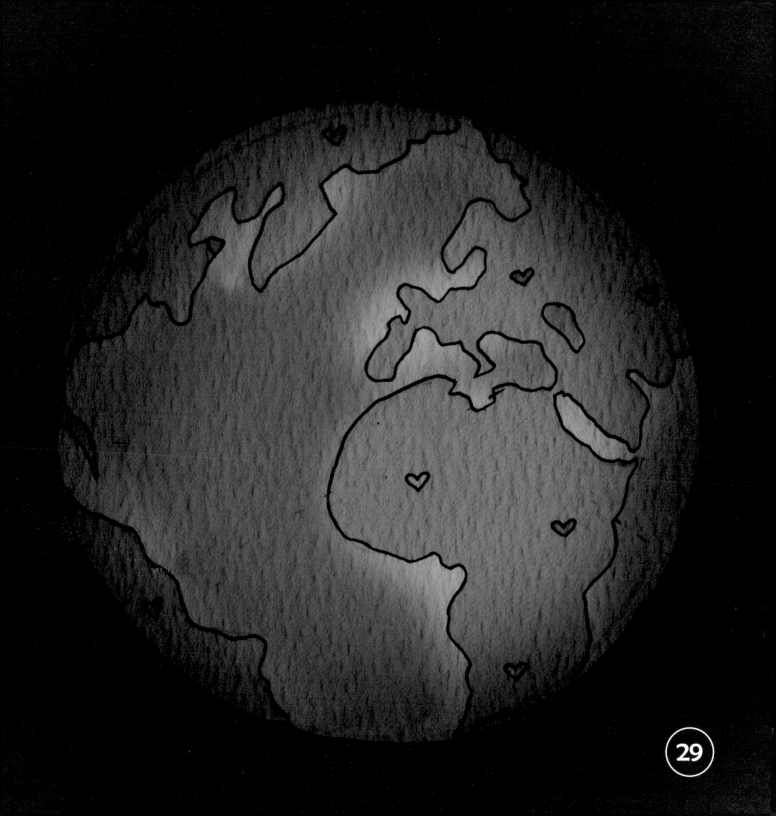

The hug sighed helplessly.

It stopped wriggling,
    stopped squirming,
        and stopped fighting.

In that moment something
magical happened.

As it stopped wriggling...
it breathed in love
and glowed brighter.

As it stopped squirming...
it remembered the heart
it was made for.

As it stopped fighting...
it slipped right past The Web
of Sticky Thoughts.

FREE!

The hug glowed
brighter and brighter...

zooming away toward
the one special heart
it was made for.

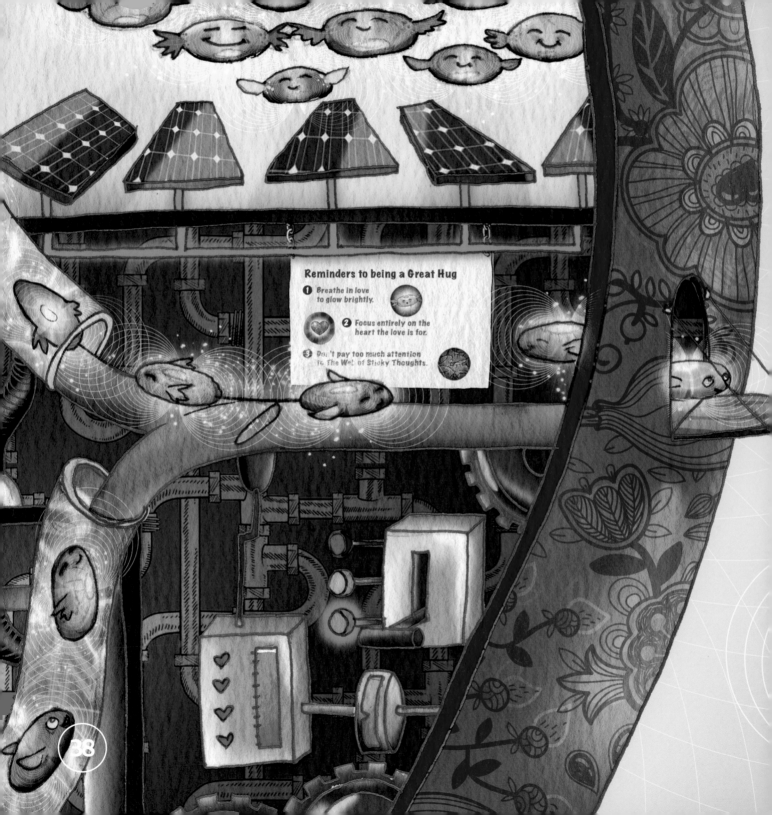

Reminders to being a Great Hug

1. Breathe in love to glow brightly.

2. Focus entirely on the heart the love is for.

3. Don't pay too much attention to the Web of Sticky Thoughts.

The Hug Factory clinked
and whirled back to life.
A flood of hugs passed in and
out of the heart, each delivering
their special love and care.

It was just one hug
who got unstuck
in the center
of one ordinary heart,
and all around the world,
an extraordinary
softening happened.

> **We need four hugs a day for survival. We need eight hugs a day for maintenance. We need twelve hugs a day for growth.**
>
> **– Virginia Satir**
> **The 'Mother of Family Therapy'**

Does your heart feel full or would you like another hug?

Have fun answering these questions together as you end your day with a full and happy heart.

Filling up on hugs

Your Daily Hug Meter

1 How many hugs did you receive today?

2 How many hugs did you give today?

URVIVE

HUG

4
3
2
1
0

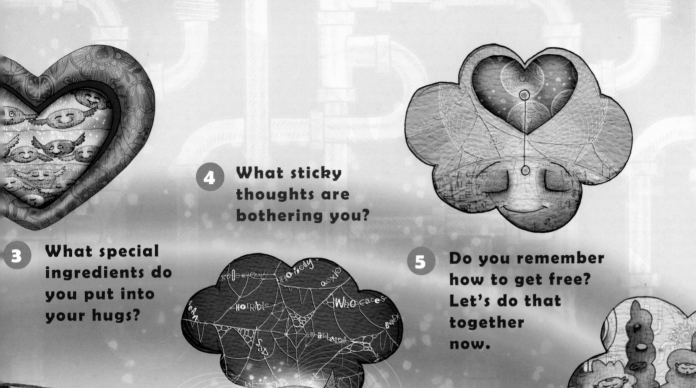

4 What sticky thoughts are bothering you?

3 What special ingredients do you put into your hugs?

5 Do you remember how to get free? Let's do that together now.

6 Who are you growing hugs for as you sleep snuggly tonight?

43

the laughing
witch

became
Spirit

Anna Breytenbach
& Andrew Newman

the tree of
goodness

Andrew Newman

Rolling Thunder
finds his herd

Andrew Newman

the elephant
who tried
to tiptoe

the dad who
didn't know

Andrew Newman

the boy who
searched
for silence

the collection

The Conscious Bedtime Story Club

snuggling into togetherness

we are circle
people

Andrew Newman

the hug who
got stuck

the fish who
searched for
water

Andrew Newman

the sunburnt
polar bear

the bee who
could not choose
her flower

Andrew Newman

a little light

the girl with
waterfall eyes

the forgetful
elephant

Andrew Newman

the prayer who
searched
for God

Andrew Newman

44

Conscious Bedtime Stories

A collection of stories with wise and lovable characters who teach spiritual values to your children

Helping you connect more deeply in the last 20 minutes of the day

Stories with purpose

Lovable characters who overcome life's challenges to find peace, love and connection.

Reflective activity pages

Cherish open sharing time with your children at the end of each day.

Simple mindfulness practices

Enjoy easy breathing practices that soften the atmosphere and create deep connection when reading together.

Supportive parenting community

Join a community of conscious parents who seek connection with their children.

Free downloadable coloring pages
Visit www.consciousstories.com

#consciousbedtimestories   @Conscious Bedtime Story Club

Andrew Newman is the award-winning author and founder of www.ConsciousStories.com, a growing series of bedtime stories purpose-built to support parent-child connection in the last 20 minutes of the day. His professional background includes deep training in therapeutic healing work and mindfulness. He brings a calm yet playful energy to speaking events and workshops, inviting and encouraging the creativity of his audiences, children K-5, parents, and teachers alike.

Andrew has been an opening speaker for Deepak Chopra, a TEDx presenter in Findhorn, Scotland and author-in-residence at the Bixby School in Boulder, Colorado. He is a graduate of The Barbara Brennan School of Healing, a Non-Dual Kabbalistic healer and has been actively involved in men's work through the Mankind Project since 2006. He counsels parents, helping them to return to their center, so they can be more deeply present with their kids.

TEDˣ **"Why the last 20 minutes of the day matter"**

Alexis Aronson – illustrator

Alexis is a self-taught illustrator, designer and artist from Cape Town, South Africa. She has a passion for serving projects with a visionary twist that incorporate image making with the growth of human consciousness for broader impact. Her media range from digital illustration and design to fine art techniques, such as intaglio printmaking, ceramic sculpture, and painting. In between working for clients and creating her own art for exhibition, Alexis is an avid nature lover, swimmer, yogi, hiker, and gardener.

www.alexisaronson.com

Star Counter

Every time you breathe together and read aloud, you make a star shine in the night sky.

Color in a star to count how many times you have read this book.